Tales of a City BY THE SEA

SAMAH SABAWI

Currency Press, Sydney

LA MAMA

CURRENT THEATRE SERIES

First published in 2016
by Currency Press Pty Ltd,
PO Box 2287, Strawberry Hills, NSW, 2012, Australia
enquiries@currency.com.au
www.currency.com.au

in association with La Mama Theatre, Melbourne.

Reprinted 2017

Cataloguing-in-publication data for this title is available from the National Library of Australia website: www.nla.gov.au

Typeset by Dean Nottle for Currency Press.
Cover image by Palestinian artist Aya El-Zinati in Gaza and Melbourne based Australian photographer Ahmad Sabra.
Cover design by Katy Wall.

Currency Press acknowledges the Traditional Owners of the Country on which we live and work. We pay our respects to all Aboriginal and Torres Strait Islander Elders, past and present.

Contents

*To my father Abdul Karim Sabawi
and his beloved city by the sea.*

ACKNOWLEDGMENTS

No words can adequately describe my sincere gratitude to Liz Jones and the La Mama staff for believing in the value of this work and for giving me unquantifiable support, starting with providing the space for our first public reading in 2012, through to co-producing our premiere in 2014 and our remount season in 2016.

A big thank you to the professional and dedicated staff of Currency Press for publishing this work and for providing a platform for new voices on the Australian theatre stage.

My deep appreciation to Daniel Clarke and Rand Hazou who guided me and mentored me every step of the way, and to Petra Kalive for her dramaturgical interventions. My love and gratitude to Steve Payne for his encouragement, guidance and friendship.

I would like to acknowledge the amazing *Tales of a City by the Sea* cast and crew both in Australia and in Palestine, with special thanks to Abdelfattah Abusrour and the Alrowwad Cultural and Theatre Society team in Aida Refugee Camp in the West Bank. Their effort to stage the play, despite the shortage of funds and in defiance of Israeli military curfews, was nothing less than inspirational.

I am indebted to Al-Qattan Centre for the Child in Gaza for hosting the public reading in 2013, and to Haidar Eid, Ayah Bashir, Eman Hilles, Sameeha Elwan, Mohammad Ghalayani, Manar Zommo, Alia Abo Oriban, Ayman Qwaider, Alaa Shublaq, Najwan Anbar, Khaled Harara, Mahmoud Hammad, Lobna El-Rayes and Salah Sabawi for their dedication to the work, their support and valuable feedback.

My appreciation and heartfelt regrets to Ali Abu Yassin and Aya El-Zinati in Gaza, whose efforts to stage the show was thwarted by the brutal war on Gaza in 2014. Those long Skype calls we shared as the bombs fell will remain etched in my memory forever.

Lots of appreciation to my sister Khulud, who is always the first to read every script I write, and to Siham, Hamed, Nahedh and Faris for putting up with me when I'm in the writing zone.

Most of all, thank you to my life partner and best friend Monir; your love nourishes my creativity and feeds my soul.

Samah Sabawi

Tales of a City by the Sea was first produced by La Mama Theatre at La Mama Courthouse, Melbourne, on 12 November 2014, with the following cast:

JOMANA	Nicole Chamoun
RAMI	Osamah Sami
LAMA	Emily Coupe
ALI	Reece Vella
ABU AHMED	Majid Shokor
SAMIRA	Wahibe Moussa
MOHANAD / HOMELAND SECURITY / FATHER IN HOSPITAL	Ubaldino Mantelli
UM AHMED / HOMELAND SECURITY / MOTHER IN HOSPITAL / NURSE	Cara Whitehouse
SINGER	Aseel Tayah

Director, Lech Mackiewicz
Assistant Director, Izabella Mackiewicz
Set Designer, Lara Week
Lighting Designer, Shane Grant
Photographer and Graphic Designer, Ahmad Sabra
Sound Designer, Khaled Sabsabi
Stage Manager, James O'Donoghue

Tales of a City by the Sea was also produced by Alrowwad Cultural and Theatre Society at Aida Refugee Camp, Palestine, on 22 November 2014, with the following cast:

JOMANA	Amira Abusrour
RAMI	Ribal AlKurdi
LAMA	Marwa Romy
ALI / HOMELAND SECURITY	Issa Mustapha
ABU AHMED	Mohamad Shalan
SAMIRA / UM AHMED (voiceover)	Hala Al-Yamani
MOHANAD / HOMELAND SECURITY	Issa Nour

Director, Abdelfattah Abusrour
Set Designers, Issa Ismael, Mahmoud Dyab and Issa Nour
Lighting and Sound Designer, Ahmed Ajarmah
Media and Publicity Co-ordinators, Mohamad Abu Hanniyah and
    Murad Abusrour

During the rehearsals and the performances in Palestine, the cast and crew were subjected to various challenges ranging from travel restrictions, to curfews and Israeli incursions into the camp. But with determination and much 'beautiful resistance', the play finally premiered nearly a week past its initial scheduled opening night.

Tales of a City by the Sea is inspired by events the author and her family have experienced during the past several years. Most of the poetry in the play was written during the three-week bombardment of Gaza in 2008/2009.

PRODUCTION NOTES

Style

Before the play begins, the cast mingles with the audience and introduces themselves as actors who are there to share a story. There is no effort to create the illusion that they are their characters. The device of Brechtian alienation emotionally separates the audience from the story to allow them to take a critical view of the action. The actors are visible at all times, when onstage and offstage. Actors who play several characters transform in full view, through costume changes, gesture, and voice.

While the story specifically takes place in 2008 during the siege of Gaza, the symbolic staging of the play does not include scenic elements that define place or time. The non-naturalistic set, composed of a set of white sheets on wires, has a makeshift sensibility. Transformations in time and place are indicated by lighting and set changes, operated by the actors as part of the action of the performance. A live singer performs traditional songs a capella in Arabic throughout these changes, punctuating the action while connecting to the audience. The play combines scenes from life with conventions of epic theatre, including direct address, poetry, and the breaking of the fourth wall.

Costumes

Characters wear simple costumes, reflective of what people in Gaza wear every day. For the most part, they are modest modern clothes, with head scarves (*hijabs*) for women characters to cover their hair. The singer, an emotional narrator for the story, has a more elaborate traditional costume.

CHARACTERS

JOMANA, a Palestinian journalist in her late twenties, born and raised in the Shati (beach) Refugee Camp in Gaza

RAMI, an American doctor of Palestinian origin in his mid thirties, born and raised in the US who came to Gaza as part of the first Free Gaza flotilla in 2008

LAMA, Jomana's cousin, a young woman in her early twenties, looking for love and adventure

ALI, a man in his late twenties who owns one of Gaza's notorious tunnels, Lama's fiancé

SAMIRA, Rami's mother, a stylish wealthy Palestinian-American woman in her late fifties, lives in the US

ABU AHMED, Jomana's father, a struggling fisherman in his late fifties, lives in Shati Refugee Camp

SINGER (optional), a woman dressed in traditional Palestinian clothes

Other minor characters:

UM AHMED, Jomana's mother

MOHANAD, Egyptian doctor coming through the tunnels

MOTHER IN HOSPITAL, mother of child who dies at hospital

FATHER IN HOSPITAL, father of child who dies at hospital

HOMELAND SECURITY OFFICER 1, at US airport

HOMELAND SECURITY OFFICER 2, at US airport

Though this play is best performed by a full cast of eight actors and a live singer, it can be performed with a minimum of six actors who can double in other roles and the singer can be substituted for an audio recording of the traditional songs named in the text.

SCENE ONE

Gaza beach.

The SINGER *stands outside of the parameters of the stage, preferably to the side where she can watch and bear witness to events. She is stationed there throughout the play.*

She sings the opening song, 'Nialak ma ahda balak' *('Lucky you have peace of mind') as the audience walks into the theatre. The sound of waves is heard in the background throughout this scene.*

On stage, JOMANA, *a woman in her late twenties, is wearing a long-sleeved shirt and jeans. Her* hijab *scarf is wrapped loosely around her shoulders. She sits on the beach with a diary in her hand and is completely absorbed in writing.* LAMA, *a young woman in her early twenties, is standing nearby looking at the sea.* LAMA *is also dressed in conservative casual clothes, but her hair is totally covered by her* hijab.

Once the audience is settled in their seats, the SINGER *stops singing and* JOMANA *begins to read from her diary.*

JOMANA: Gaza, August 2008
 The landscape constantly changes
 Only the sea remains
 Salty
 Fluid
 Mysterious
 Moody
 A consistent presence amid the chaos—

> *The sound of an Israeli drone interrupts* JOMANA. *She looks up at the sky and follows the drone with her eyes until the sound fades out. She returns to her diary.*

Its whooshing waves whisper tales
Of occupiers that have come and gone
Crusaders, tyrants and warlords
Riding on their horses
Riding on their tanks
Riding on their F-16 fighter jets

Always riding through
Leaving their footprints
And part of their history
Leaving their artefacts and ruins
Leaving fire and debris
Always leaving …
Only the sea remains.

LAMA: I love coming here.

JOMANA: I know.

LAMA: If you stand with your back to Gaza, facing the sea, you can easily imagine you are someplace else: Beirut … Alexandria … Tripoli … Santorini …

JOMANA: Countries … continents … the whole world is out there.

> LAMA *sits next to* JOMANA. *They stare silently into the sea.*

LAMA: If only we could ride the sea.

JOMANA: If only our bodies were bulletproof.

LAMA: If only our boats were made of steel.

JOMANA: If only our dreams were real.

> *Pause.*

Look! You can see the Free Gaza boats from here.

LAMA: They must be ready to leave. You know, I stayed up all night fantasising about sneaking on board these boats. Imagine me … an adventurous stowaway sailing off to see the world.

JOMANA: Sure … on what passport?

LAMA: I said stowaway … must you ruin every fantasy?

JOMANA: Fantasies get stuck at the borders; they never make it past the checkpoints.

LAMA: Well, a few fantasies must have snuck on board these boats because I'm having them.

> *Faint sound of music in the distance.*

JOMANA: Really?

LAMA: Music!

JOMANA: What more will they do for these activists?

LAMA: Oh, how exciting! This is the most entertainment we've had here in years.

JOMANA's *phone beeps; she reads a text message, smiles and texts back.*

Who are you texting?

JOMANA: One of my many admirers of course! Listen, why don't you go to the pier and take a closer look at the action? I know you're dying to.

LAMA: Only if you come with me!

JOMANA: I want to finish writing this poem and you are distracting me.

LAMA: You can write this poem some other time! Come on! Maybe we'll be lucky and make it on the news tonight.

JOMANA: I wouldn't want to steal the show from the activists.

LAMA: You won't have to … the politicians have stolen the show a long time ago, with all the speeches and photo ops. Come on! We are the people … we too deserve our share of the spotlight.

JOMANA: Fascinating! Girls your age dream of being discovered by film producers or modelling agencies and you dream of being discovered by news networks.

LAMA: This is Gaza; we make do with whatever we have.

JOMANA: I guess. Our entire life seems to be one long news story!

LAMA: Oh, lighten up! *Yallah*, come with me. I want to watch the dancing.

JOMANA's *phone beeps again; she checks the text message and smiles.* LAMA *looks at her with suspicion.*

Oh, my God! This smile …

JOMANA: What?

LAMA: I haven't seen this smile before. This is new. Jomana, who are you texting?

LAMA *reaches for the phone but* JOMANA *quickly sticks it in her pocket.*

JOMANA: This is none of your business. But you know what is your business? Your fiancé Ali! Why don't you go and find him? After all, you're supposed to be with him, not with me.

LAMA: You want me to find Ali? Let me tell you: Ali is inevitability. He is like death. It doesn't matter where I hide from him, he will find me.

JOMANA: You are terrible!

ALI *arrives holding two juice cups. He is wearing dress pants and a shirt and has a cigarette tucked behind his ear.*

ALI: There you are!

LAMA: Told you!

> ALI *hands* LAMA *and* JOMANA *the juice. He kneels next to* LAMA.

ALI: [*pretending to whisper*] Okay, let me try to explain how this is supposed to work … You and I are supposed to ditch the chaperone. Yet, every time I've taken you out, you and your chaperone end up ditching me.

LAMA: Oh, Ali, a little effort is not going to kill you! You're supposed to chase after me, so do your job and stop whining.

ALI: I don't mind chasing, but today, with all the international media, I thought it would make good PR for Gaza to have a gorgeous couple like us walking around … holding hands …

> ALI *leans over closer to* LAMA *flirtatiously,. She pushes him away and he falls.* JOMANA *laughs.*

JOMANA: Yes, Lama, you should totally do it for Gaza.

ALI: Damn right she should! How else can we humanise the men in this place?

LAMA: Fine! I will be a martyr for the cause. I will come with you, hold your hand and look at you with adoring eyes, but this act will cost you much more than a juice cup, Romeo.

ALI: Name your price.

LAMA: Dinner at The Lighthouse.

ALI: Done.

JOMANA: Great! Off you go. This chaperone would love nothing more than to be ditched by both of you. *Yallah*, leave before I change my mind.

> ALI *stands up, offers* LAMA *a hand and pulls her up.*

ALI: Let's hurry. I promised Rami to meet him at the pier.

> JOMANA *hides a smile.* ALI *and* LAMA *don't notice.*

LAMA: Hang on. Let me fix my *hijab*.

> *She tightens her scarf around her head.*

Jomana, are you sure you don't want to come?

JOMANA: Positive! I'll catch up with you later.

LAMA: Fine. But please cover your hair if you plan to stay here by yourself. You are not in Europe, you know.

JOMANA: But you said I could imagine I am someplace else.

LAMA: Ha-ha …

>   ALI *pulls* LAMA *away.* LAMA *yells as she leaves.*

Seriously, you can't sit alone looking like this! Cover your hair! You know how strict they've become about these things!

>   JOMANA *stands up and reaches for her scarf reluctantly as she watches them leave; then in a deliberate move, she lets go of it and begins to fix her hair, mumbling to herself.*

JOMANA: Oh, they won't be strict today. They want to show the world how progressive they are …

>   RAMI *enters, but* JOMANA *doesn't see him, she continues talking to herself. He stands right behind her, wearing rolled-up, worn-out jeans, a* keffieh, *sandals with socks and a backpack covered with Palestine solidarity badges and stickers.* JOMANA *continues ...*

… After all, the guests they are bidding farewell to are a bunch of non-*hijab* wearing feminists, lefties and gays …

RAMI: And which category do I fall into?

JOMANA: [*startled*] Rami!

RAMI: Well?

JOMANA: Let me see … I think you are the tormented diaspora Palestinian who wears Palestine as if it were a fashion statement … but there is hope for you.

>   RAMI *walks closer to her, staring in total adoration.*

RAMI: And hope is what sustains me. I'm so glad you came!

JOMANA: I'm on chaperone duty. I had to come.

>   RAMI *gently strokes her face with his fingers. Shyly she steps away from his reach. He looks at her diary book.*

RAMI: What are you writing?

JOMANA: A new poem.

RAMI: I look forward to reading it.

>   RAMI *steps closer, but* JOMANA *backs away nervously.*

JOMANA: Do you see the port? The circus is over *there*.

RAMI: I only see you.

JOMANA: Music, balloons and *debka*.

RAMI: Time went by quickly. I can't believe I've only been here for six days. I don't know how I will leave this place.

JOMANA: Then don't. Don't leave! It was a miracle that you even made it in in the first place.

RAMI: I know. We made history! We broke the siege for the first time!

JOMANA: And did it on two small wooden boats …

RAMI: Impressive, right?

JOMANA: Is this the part where I'm supposed to melt?

> *They share a smile, but* JOMANA*'s smile doesn't last long. She turns her back to* RAMI, *looking increasingly sad.*

I heard one guy from Italy decided to stay.

RAMI: Yes. Vittorio. He is lucky he can do that.

JOMANA: He is? So why not you? This is your homeland. You should be the one staying here. You shouldn't have to run back to America.

RAMI: So you want me to stay?

JOMANA: I don't care what you do, I'm only pointing out what your duty is to your country … you know … from purely a nationalistic point of view. Gaza needs you. That's all!

RAMI: Believe me, Jomana, I need her too. I think I've fallen in love … with her.

JOMANA: Really? … But you hardly know her.

> RAMI *holds* JOMANA*'s hand.*

RAMI: I have known her all my life.

> *He kisses her hand. She blushes and quickly pulls away. He looks around.*

You know, I think this is it. This is the exact spot where my grandparents took a photo of their first outing together. It was back in 1954. My grandfather was dressed in his best suit and *tarbush*, and my grandmother looked like a Hollywood movie star. My grandfather stood behind her like this …

> RAMI *stands behind* JOMANA.

… and he had one hand on her waist, like this.

> RAMI *tries to put his hand on* JOMANA*'s waist. She looks around nervously and quickly removes it.*

I never thought I'd come here and stand in this spot … with a love of my own… I love you, Jomana!

JOMANA: Then don't leave! Please don't leave!

RAMI: My patients … my clinic … my interns … my mother … I have things I must do in the US. Too many people are waiting for me. But I promise you I will sort things out and will come back.

JOMANA: Please, just don't! Don't make promises you can't keep. How and why would you come back? There is nothing here for you.

RAMI: Not even from a nationalistic point of view?

>JOMANA *is not amused.*

There is plenty for me here. My heart is here. My everything is right here.

JOMANA: Don't call me your 'everything' and in the same breath tell me you have to go.

RAMI: I will return.

JOMANA: How? We're under siege.

RAMI: Look over there at these two wooden boats. They sailed rough seas, stood up to one of the world's most powerful armies and made it here. They … we … broke the siege. The boats will come back and I will come back.

JOMANA: Beautiful words, but all I hear is you saying goodbye … I'm so stupid. I'm so stupid.

>*She begins to wrap her* hijab *around her head, covering her hair.*

I really thought I could convince you to stay.

RAMI: I wish I could … I really do … but I just can't drop my entire life … Jomana, what has gotten into you?

JOMANA: Don't you get it? Over here, every time we say goodbye to someone, we say it like it is the last time, and most often this turns out to be the case. No-one can get in … *We can't get out!*

RAMI: Don't be so dramatic.

JOMANA: *Dramatic?! Ya allah!* What was I thinking?

>*She tries to leave; he pulls her back.*

RAMI: Jomana, wait … I don't understand …

JOMANA: But I do! I've seen your type many times before.

RAMI: What is that supposed to mean?

JOMANA: You know … your type. Palestinians with international passports … they come here on a feel-good adventure to see the poor people of Gaza. They take photos, make promises, and then they run back home to their comfortable lives where once in a while they talk about the plight of their people over polite dinner conversations with other sophisticated privileged people …

RAMI: You can't be serious …

JOMANA: Perhaps your friends will be entertained to know that on top of our poverty and terrible living conditions we also seem to suffer from irrational and *dramatic* separation anxiety.

RAMI: What the fuck is the matter with you?

JOMANA: Don't use that disgusting American language here.

RAMI: Don't tell me what language I can or cannot use. You think this is a hobby? You think I'm on a search for entertaining topics for dinner conversations? You really think that the Free Gaza boats are some kind of adventure tourism? Is this what you think of me? Is this what you think of the activists who risked their lives for you, for us, for our people?

JOMANA: Oh, please … 'our people'? Look at us! Look at where I live. Then think of your life. Rami, there is no 'our people'. There is *my* people and then there is *your* people!

RAMI: So you get to decide if I am Palestinian or not? Jomana, I came here to make a difference, to stand up for what I believe in and to reconnect with my roots and you know what, I admit it. *Yes! I feel good about it!* I don't have to apologise for that. In fact I don't have to apologise for being born in the US or for having a decent and secure life there.

JOMANA: Well, I've lived here all my life and I am trapped and insecure and tired of being abandoned by those who leave and never return.

RAMI: It is tearing me up to have to leave, but you must understand that I am not running away.

He pulls her in and holds her hands.

I am not running away. I couldn't do that even if I tried.

JOMANA: I just … feel as though I've waited for you all my life … and now that you're here I'm supposed to watch you leave …

RAMI: I've waited for you too. For so many years, I've read your blogs, your poems, every letter you've written … every word … every sentence drew me in deeper and deeper. I have fallen in love with you even before I set foot in Gaza. I cannot imagine a life without you.

JOMANA: I too have kept every email you've sent ... memorised every word ... tried to imagine what it would be like if you came here ... God! I was so naïve to think that you'd take one breath here and feel so at home that you would never want to leave.

RAMI: *Habibty*, I love you! ... Let's not fight anymore. I don't want our last time together to be like this. Have faith in me when I say I will return. I promise! I promise!

The SINGER *sings the heartache song,* 'El Asmar al loon', *as the couple walk away from one another.*

The lights fade out and the singing continues until the start of the next scene.

SCENE TWO

Split stage.

On one side JOMANA *and* LAMA *are sitting in Jomana's living room in the Shati Camp on a modest sofa with a simple coffee table and Palestinian-embroidered cushions. There is an open laptop on the coffee table. The two girls are laughing.*

On the other side RAMI *is sitting on a lush leather sofa in his upscale southern US home looking into his laptop. Throughout the scene* JOMANA's *mother,* UM AHMED's, *voice is heard from the kitchen.*

UM AHMED: [*off*] What are you two giggling about? Enough nonsense and come to the kitchen.

LAMA: *Khalto*, I'm telling Jomana a very juicy story. Just give us a few minutes.

JOMANA: Well? Don't leave me hanging. What did Salim say?

LAMA: My poor brother ... [*Laughing*] When her father opened the door, he had no choice but to pretend he was actually visiting him and not coming to see Dalya.

JOMANA: That's hilarious!

LAMA: Her father looked a little suspicious, so Salim had to pretend he was a fan of his poetry.

JOMANA: [*hysterically laughing now*] Oh, no ... not the poetry ...

LAMA: Yes ... the poetry ... So ... Salim spent the night with Dalya's father listening to really bad poetry and pretending to enjoy it.

JOMANA: Tell me at least Dalya was there.

LAMA: That's the best part. She wasn't. She was at our house ... looking for Salim. When she saw me she pretended she came to see me. Thinking Salim would be back soon, I tried to hold on to her for as long as I could. We watched a movie then we played cards ... When she finally gave up and headed for the door Salim came home. By then it was too late and she didn't want to make it obvious, so she left.

JOMANA: That's just too funny ... don't they know it already *is* obvious ...?

LAMA: I know ... aren't they the sorriest lovebirds in Gaza ...?

The Skype phone rings. JOMANA *looks at* LAMA.

JOMANA: [*pleading*] Please!

LAMA *gives her a stern look.*

LAMA: Why is he calling you? Jomana, this relationship will never work. Don't answer.

JOMANA: I wish it were that easy. I'm in love with him.

The Skype phone continues to ring, punctuated by the mother's voice calling from the kitchen.

UM AHMED: [*off*] Jomana ... Lama ...

RAMI: Jomana ... please pick up.

JOMANA: Please, Lama, cover for me. Think of all the times I covered for you. Am I not always the best chaperone you can ever dream of? Please ...

UM AHMED: [*off*] What is this ringing?

LAMA: Nothing, *Khalto*, I'm coming to help now.

LAMA *gives* JOMANA *one last look of disapproval then leaves.* JOMANA *quickly fixes her hair and pinches her cheeks, then answers the Skype call.*

RAMI: Finally! I worried you wouldn't answer.

JOMANA: I had to convince Lama to leave us alone.

RAMI: And we know how much she likes me.

JOMANA: She can be a little overprotective.

RAMI: Well, she needs to get off my case, and dedicate her time to doing what she does best: tormenting Ali.

JOMANA: Are you really going to waste this call complaining about Lama?

RAMI: No! I would much rather tell you how beautiful you look and that I love you. I love you. I love you. I can't wait to hold you again.

JOMANA: I miss you.

RAMI: I heard a suitor is coming your way in the next couple of weeks.

JOMANA: Where did you hear that?

RAMI: I know him very well. He is an amazing catch.

JOMANA: Rami, how could you say that?

RAMI: He is good for you. He is a handsome doctor from a good family. That is like the top of the suitor ladder for Palestinians worldwide.

JOMANA: I see … What if I still refuse him?

RAMI: Nonsense! He is the best.

JOMANA: Really?

RAMI: Ask my mother. She'll tell you how great he is.

JOMANA: Really? You're coming in a few weeks?

RAMI: Yes.

JOMANA: But the Rafah crossing is shut? How will you get in?

RAMI: My mother has some impressive connections she will put to good use.

JOMANA: I don't know what to say. I can't believe you are coming back. You will stay this time, won't you?

RAMI: [*hesitating slightly*] … Yes.

JOMANA: I have to tell my parents. They don't know about you yet. There is so much to do. I am so happy. Oh, my God … you're coming back!

RAMI: And word has it we are going to be the hottest couple in Gaza.

JOMANA: I'm sure the cameras will follow us around for days.

RAMI: Yes … they will call us Ramana.

JOMANA: Ramana? What does that mean?

RAMI: You know … Rami and Jomana … like Brangelina.

JOMANA: What is a Brangelina?

RAMI: Never mind. It is an American thing.

JOMANA: I don't understand, but speaking of American, you need to make sure you dress less American and more Palestinian when you come this time.

RAMI: Now I'm the one that can't understand.

JOMANA: It's just that no-one here believes you are a real doctor. Torn jeans … really Rami? You looked like a pauper. This stuff just doesn't work here. You have to make some major adjustments, get a haircut and wear a nice cardigan. Oh, yeah … and never ever wear socks with sandals. That's just forbidden.

RAMI: Do I need to adjust my medical skills too?

JOMANA: Yes, of course. They need to be more suited to the conditions at the Gaza hospitals.

RAMI: So learn how to operate without anaesthetics.

JOMANA: And treat cancer patients while smoking cigarettes.

RAMI: And lecture diabetics while offering them sweet pastry.

JOMANA: And perform surgeries without electricity.

> *A knock on the door* … JOMANA *panics.*

> *Baba* is home.

>> JOMANA*'s father,* ABU AHMED, *enters just as she shuts off her laptop and stands up.* RAMI *remains seated on the other side with a big smile on his face.* JOMANA *walks over and kisses her father's hand. He holds her hand in his and kisses her on her forehead.*

> How was your day *Baba*? Any luck fishing?

ABU AHMED: The army shot at our boat. This time they damaged the engine. We didn't get too far.

>> JOMANA *helps her father out of his coat.*

>> *Meanwhile, on the other side* RAMI*'s mother* SAMIRA *enters with shopping bags. She is dressed elegantly in a knee-high, sleeveless dress and meticulous short hair. She is a beautiful, stylish, middle-aged woman.* RAMI *looks up and smiles as she walks over and kisses him on the head.*

SAMIRA: I thought if I went to the farmers' market early I would avoid the crowd, but it was packed! Still, I managed to buy everything we need for Thanksgiving.

RAMI: Wonderful! You always cook an amazing feast.

>> RAMI *carries the shopping bags into the kitchen.* SAMIRA *plunges herself on the sofa, kicks off her shoes, puts her feet up and shuts her eyes.*

JOMANA *brings her father his house slippers.*

JOMANA: What about the human rights boat with the Italian guy that sailed with you?

ABU AHMED: They shot at his boat too.

JOMANA: Is he alright?

ABU AHMED: Yes, *habibty*, he is. He picked up some really good Arabic swear words and put them to good use.

JOMANA: [*laughing*] Vittorio is truly amazing!

ABU AHMED: Every time I start to lose sight of what is good in this world, I think of him and others like him who have given up comfortable lives to come here and to stand by our side.

The lights go out in Jomana's living room.

It seems every day we get less electricity than the day before.

ABU AHMED *takes out a lighter from his pocket and lights it so he can find his way to the sofa in the dark.* JOMANA *walks into the kitchen.*

RAMI: [*from the kitchen*] How many people are we expecting?

SAMIRA: Not many … *ya alby* … maybe fifteen!

RAMI: [*from the kitchen*] Coffee?

SAMIRA: Yes please!

LAMA *comes in with a lantern; she places it on the table and gives* ABU AHMED *a hug.*

LAMA: *Merhaba, Ammu.*

ABU AHMED: *Ahleen*, my favourite niece. As much as I love seeing you here, I have the feeling you should be at home right now. Isn't Ali invited there for dinner?

JOMANA *comes out of the kitchen carrying a* sheesha *and places it in front of her father. She begins to massage his shoulders.*

JOMANA: That explains why she's here.

ABU AHMED: Lama, you can't treat the man this way. No-one is forcing you to marry him, so you either break up with him or you set the date for the wedding. You can't string him along forever.

LAMA: I know … I know … I know … but a bird in one hand … a geeky bird with no sense of style, but still …

ABU AHMED: Lama, shame on you!

LAMA: I'm kidding … I will go once I'm done helping *Khalto* in the kitchen.

> LAMA *walks back into the kitchen.* ABU AHMED *begins smoking his* sheesha, *thoroughly enjoying it.*

ABU AHMED: It's a shame no-one has come up with a way for us to use our water pipes to generate electricity. With all the *sheesha* smokers in Gaza we can light up the entire Middle East.

> RAMI *enters with two coffee mugs. He puts one on the table and hands* SAMIRA *the other one. She sits up.*

SAMIRA: Can you turn down the aircon, *ya alby*, it is freezing here?

> RAMI *grabs the remote control and turns down the air conditioner.*

RAMI: What are you planning to make for dessert?

SAMIRA: Not sure yet … let me see, *kunafa, baklava* …

RAMI: Mom, this is Thanksgiving, not *Eid.*

SAMIRA: I was only pulling your leg. Of course you'll get your pumpkin pie … you always get your pumpkin pie. You know there is no Thanksgiving in Gaza, don't you? No pumpkin pie … no cranberry sauce … no stuffing … no gravy … no basics … hell … no water … no … electricity …

ABU AHMED: Only four hours of electricity a day! I think the Israelis want to push us back into the Dark Ages.

LAMA: [*from the kitchen*] Speaking of the Dark Ages, Ammu, the water has run out.

ABU AHMED: I'll call the water truck to refill.

SAMIRA: I just remembered, make sure you tell Piedro to clean the pool and turn the heater on. Your sister's kids will want to swim. This will probably be their last swim for the season.

ABU AHMED: [*calling off*] Um Ahmed, take it easy with the water, you have to make it last longer!

UM AHMED: [*off*] It's not like I'm bathing in it. Why don't you bring me some stones and I can just rub them against the pots like they did thousands of years ago.

ABU AHMED: [*calling off*] They didn't use pots thousands of years ago!

UM AHMED: [*off*] That's not a bad idea. Maybe I shouldn't use pots either. You can live on salad from now on.

ABU AHMED: [*whispering to* JOMANA] Sometimes your mother's tyranny exceeds that of the Israeli army's.

UM AHMED: [*off*] I heard that.

> JOMANA *and* ABU AHMED *laugh.*

SAMIRA: I got a call from Abu Emad today. He said we have a good chance of getting into Gaza. But it is not one hundred percent guaranteed.

RAMI: How much do we need to pay him?

SAMIRA: Two thousand dollars for the both of us.

RAMI: Bloody thieves!

JOMANA: *Baba*, what will you do with the boat?

ABU AHMED: I have to borrow some money again to fix it.

SAMIRA: The money is the easy part.

ABU AHMED: But there is something else that is on my mind?

SAMIRA: I'm worried about you.

ABU AHMED: Why did my daughter greet me at the door, bring me my slippers, make me a *sheesha* and even offer a massage?

> JOMANA *seems nervous.*

Is there something we need to talk about?

SAMIRA: We need to talk about this.

JOMANA: [*taking a deep breath*] Remember in August …

SAMIRA: When you went on the boats.

JOMANA: When the boats came in.

SAMIRA: I was so proud of you, *ya alby*, for doing something that is good for our people.

ABU AHMED: That was a proud day. How can I forget it? No-one in Gaza can forget that day.

JOMANA: Do you remember the Palestinian doctor that came on one of the boats?

ABU AHMED: What doctor?

SAMIRA: That was my son, born and raised his whole life in Texas, living a life of comfort, having achieved the highest levels of education.

ABU AHMED: The only Palestinian I remember was an American hippie in torn jeans and sandals with socks.

SAMIRA: That was Dr Rami … giving back to his people and taking on a brave journey. If your dad were alive he would have been so proud of you.

JOMANA: *Baba*, in America, doctors don't really care how they look.

RAMI: Strange to hear you say this now, Mom, seeing you didn't approve of me going on the Free Gaza boats.

ABU AHMED: Hum … And you, my child, do you care how he looks?

SAMIRA: I worried about you. You were running back into what we ran away from.

JOMANA: *Baba!* He is coming with his mother in two weeks. He would like to drink a cup of coffee with you.

SAMIRA: Now I'm even more worried. I mean, you're not going this time on a short humanitarian mission …

ABU AHMED: He's coming all the way from America with his mother, and once again wants to break through the siege to drink coffee with me? I am flattered!

RAMI: Mom, I know this is difficult.

JOMANA: *Baba*, stop teasing me. You know what I mean.

ABU AHMED: I do. *Habibty*, I have to be honest with you …

SAMIRA: It is beyond difficult. It is hard for me to accept.

ABU AHMED: I'm not sure I like this.

JOMANA: *Baba*, he is a good man … a doctor.

RAMI: Mom, she is an incredible educated woman.

ABU AHMED: He has American citizenship.

SAMIRA: She is a stateless refugee.

ABU AHMED: His feet aren't rooted in this soil.

SAMIRA: She is trapped in Gaza.

ABU AHMED: He has wings and the freedom to leave when things get tough here.

SAMIRA: You will lose your freedom and be trapped if you stay with her.

ABU AHMED: What if he takes you with him to America? I would never see you again.

SAMIRA: I would never see you again.

ABU AHMED: Your sister lives in the West Bank, a stone's throw away, but she may as well be living on the moon.

SAMIRA: Look at how hard it is for us to go there now.

ABU AHMED: We have tried for years to get permission from Israel to allow us to visit each other and you know what that's like.

SAMIRA: Impossible … it would be impossible to visit you … or see your children.

ABU AHMED: She has three children who only know me as a virtual grandfather that speaks to them from inside a computer screen.

RAMI: Don't worry, Mom. I may be able to convince her to leave Gaza eventually and to come to live here with us.

JOMANA: Don't worry, *Baba*, I told him I would never leave you. He promised me he would stay in Gaza.

SAMIRA: You weren't honest with her?

ABU AHMED: And you believe him?

SAMIRA: You need to tell her you may not stay there.

RAMI: Then she will refuse to marry me.

JOMANA: I want to believe him.

RAMI: I wasn't being dishonest. I just don't know. Maybe there is a place for me in Gaza. Maybe that is God's plan for me and I just don't know it.

JOMANA: He asked me to have faith in him.

ABU AHMED: How will he get in? Israel is turning back the boats now and all the crossings into Egypt are shut.

RAMI: I don't have all the answers, but I know I have to be with her.

JOMANA: Connections. He said he knows some people high up in the Palestinian Authority.

RAMI: Can't we just take it one step at a time?

SAMIRA: One step at a time?

ABU AHMED: He is counting on the Palestinian Authority?

SAMIRA: We don't even know we can make it in.

ABU AHMED: Even the president of the Palestinian Authority needs permission from Israel first and at times it can be denied.

> JOMANA *looks very sad.* RAMI *is agitated by* SAMIRA*'s words. Both parents feel bad and try to console their children.*

SAMIRA: I am sorry, *ya alby*, if I upset you.

ABU AHMED: Don't worry, *habibty. Inshallah*, God will bring what is best.

SAMIRA: I'll try to be positive. What is meant to be, will be.

ABU AHMED: If you're meant to marry him, you will. Let's put our faith in God's hands.

RAMI: Mom, can I have your blessing?

JOMANA: *Baba*, do we have your blessing?

ABU AHMED: You always have my blessing.

SAMIRA: Always!

> *The* SINGER *sings the parents' song,* 'Ya khayee qool laommy we la tqool laboya'.
>
> *The lights fade and the* SINGER*'s voice continues into the start of the next scene.*

SCENE THREE

Split stage.

One side is dark.

On the other side RAMI *is in a furnished apartment in Cairo. He stands with his eyes glued on* SAMIRA *who is pacing back and forth while holding a phone to her ear.*

SAMIRA: But … Wait … Okay. Yes, I know … We tried that already. What else …? Sure … *Tayeb* … *Tayeb* … *Khalas* … *Shokran*.

> SAMIRA *puts her phone down and turns to* RAMI. *She shakes her head.* RAMI*'s anger explodes. He slams his fist against the disk.*

RAMI: No.

SAMIRA: I am sorry, *ya alby*, this was God's will. There is nothing we can do about it.

RAMI: Let's leave God out of this one.

SAMIRA: We did everything we could.

RAMI: I am so sick of this. Fuck! I am so sick of this … I'd try the boats again but there is no use … Israel is now turning those away. I want to see her. I have to get back in. I promised her to return …

SAMIRA: Perhaps this is one promise you shouldn't have made. You can't promise something that is not in your hands to give. You have to understand that you both live in separate worlds.

RAMI: This is not helping right now. I should have stayed …! She was right, I should have stayed … She knew this was going to happen … I called her 'dramatic'—can you believe?—what a fucking moron I was … She was right all along. I should have stayed.

SAMIRA: Just like that? Dropped everything you've worked your entire life for? Then what? I have to tell you my heart ached when I thought you would be living—even if for a short period of time—behind those walls. It is not a place I want to see my grandchildren being raised. I probably wouldn't be allowed to see them at all.

RAMI: Mom, please … just stop.

> SAMIRA *shakes her head exasperated, but decides to say nothing more and walks away.* RAMI *buries his face in his hands.*

> *The lights go on on the other side.* JOMANA *sits in her living room. She is wearing a beautiful dress and her hair is done up with small flowers in it. She wipes a tear off her face, grabs her diary and begins to write:*

JOMANA: Gaza, December 2008

Are your loved ones trapped behind the wall
Do they need the army's permission
For their prayers to reach the sky
For their love to cross the ocean
And to touch your thirsty heart
Are your loved ones trapped?

> RAMI *turns on his laptop and calls* JOMANA. *Her Skype phone rings. She drops her diary and quickly grabs her laptop.*

RAMI: Jomana, please pick up …

JOMANA: Hey, you! At last!

RAMI: You look beautiful.

JOMANA: I got all dressed up for you. I even had my hair done up.

RAMI: They wouldn't let us in.

JOMANA: When I heard the Egyptians turned you back, I didn't have the heart to take off the dress or to let my hair down! I thought at least you could see me on Skype … I mean, after all of this effort.

RAMI: You look incredible! Just wow!

JOMANA: I'm sure it's not every day that a woman spends hours beautifying herself for you.

RAMI: Definitely not every day. Only once or twice a week usually!

JOMANA: Lucky you!

RAMI: You have no idea what seeing you look like this is doing to me! I would die just to touch you. I want to fly through their damned borders, sit beside you, and pull these flowers out of your hair, one little flower at a time. I want to watch you move. I hold my breath every time your shawl slides down your arms … My heart stops at the thought of holding your hand in mine. You take my breath away, Jomana … You really shouldn't have shown me how amazing you look tonight … You have no mercy!

JOMANA: I could turn off the camera.

RAMI: *No* …! Better yet, how about you stand up? Let me have a look at your dress.

> JOMANA *stands and takes a few steps away from the computer. She twirls so he can see the back and front of her dress.* RAMI *watches her with a sad smile filled with desire.*

I want to hold you.

JOMANA: I want to hide in your arms.

RAMI: Don't give up on me.

JOMANA: Promise me you'll never stop trying.

> *They both share a silent moment staring into the screen.*

How is your mom?

RAMI: The drive to Rafah was hard and the waiting even harder …

JOMANA: I can imagine.

RAMI: But she is a strong woman.

JOMANA: And you?

RAMI: I'm broken.

> *Faint sounds of shelling commence in the distance and remain throughout the rest of this scene.*

JOMANA: And so begins our nightly lullabies …

RAMI: They seem to be a bit louder tonight.

JOMANA: I know. Rami, I can't wait anymore. I want to tell you now … I love you! There, I've said it.

RAMI: Finally! I thought I'd never hear you utter these words.

JOMANA: I wanted to say it to your face. But it seems we are condemned to a Skype love affair.

RAMI: I am starting to worry we might end up getting married and having babies on Skype.

JOMANA: That's a scary thought. I'd better sign off then, before I find myself pregnant.

RAMI: Noooo, don't go!

JOMANA: I'm sorry, *habibty*. It is really late. *Yallah*, goodnight!
RAMI: Goodnight, *habibty*, I love you.

> *The lights go out on both sides. The sound of shelling gradually becomes louder. This goes on for a couple of minutes.*

> *When the lights come back on,* JOMANA *is sitting on her sofa wearing casual clothes. She seems frightened. She is writing into her diary.*

JOMANA: Gaza
December 27, 2008
I search ... desperately ... for words ...
I have no words ...
I have no words ...

> *The sound of a loud explosion close by.* JOMANA *jumps in fear, dropping her diary.*

[*Shouting angrily*] *I need new words!*

> *Determined, she picks up her diary.*

Siege ... hunger ... collective misery
Familiar words in my head, they linger
Bombs fall from the sky every day
Powerless words ...
Powerless words ...
I can't use any longer
I need new words—

> *A loud explosion is heard this time, with the sounds of glass shattering.* ABU AHMED *enters, alarmed.* JOMANA *runs to him.*

Baba!

ABU AHMED: Everyone is fine, but we must leave now. Just grab your things and let's go fast.
JOMANA: But ... our home ... *Baba*. Where do we go?
ABU AHMED: I don't know, but it is definitely not safe here.

> JOMANA *packs a few items quickly: the diary, the pen, her scarf. She is getting her coat.*

> *On the other side of the stage the lights go on.* RAMI *is on his computer looking horrified. He calls* JOMANA *on Skype. She is about*

to pack the last item, her laptop, when the Skype phone rings. She looks at her father, pleading. He nods.

Make it fast. I'll take these things to the car.

The sound of shelling continues louder.

JOMANA: Rami, we've been through many bombings, but this is the worst. There are people, bodies … children … death everywhere, Rami … I can't speak. I can't put it in words. I have no words. I have no words. We have to leave the house. The shelling is very heavy at the camp. I don't know where our families will go. We'll be out of touch for a while. Pray for us. Pray for us.

A loud noise sounds, like missiles falling. The light on JOMANA*'s side of the stage goes out.*

RAMI: Jomana … Jomana … Jomana … Damn … Connection lost.

He grabs his mobile phone and dials.

Ali, I've decided to join you. Please make the necessary arrangement.

SAMIRA *enters alarmed.*

SAMIRA: What was that about?

RAMI: Mom, I have to go.

SAMIRA: No … no … no …

RAMI: I'm not going alone.

SAMIRA: No … *ya allah!* … No!

RAMI: There is a group of Egyptian doctors who are going. My friend Dr Mustafa tells me the hospitals are overwhelmed with the injured. They need our help. Israel and Egypt won't allow people through the normal channels. No-one is allowed in or out of Gaza … you know that. So we have to do what we can to get there.

SAMIRA *collapses on the chair sobbing.* RAMI *goes down on his knees.*

The hospitals were already short of everything, because of the siege. Mom, I was trained to save lives. I can't sit and watch. We will be taking critical medical supplies with us. The tunnel we're using is one of the best and safest.

He kisses her hand.

Mom, please … I need your blessing.

SAMIRA *stares at her son with tears streaming down her face.*

Beat.

She tries to get up.

SAMIRA: Let me pack you some food.

RAMI: It is not a good idea. There are no toilets in the tunnel and we'll need to crawl for hours underground. We were advised to keep our stomachs and bladders light.

SAMIRA: Ah, *ya alby!* The places you go!

RAMI *smiles tenderly.*

RAMI: I have brains in my head.

I have feet in my shoes

SAMIRA: You still remember …

RAMI: Dr Seuss! It was our sacred bedtime ritual for years.

SAMIRA: You were such a typical American boy! But now this.

SAMIRA *and* RAMI *recite 'Oh, the Places You'll Go' by Dr Seuss.*

Ah, *ya alby!* When will I see you again?

The SINGER *begins to sing the farewell to mother song, 'Ala tareeq ghaza ya ommy'.*

RAMI *and his mother embrace. He kisses her hands and her face and starts to walk away.*

The lights fade and the SINGER *continues the song into the next scene.*

SCENE FOUR

Gaza tunnel city.

The stage is bare with a white tent at the centre. ALI *stands outside the tent facing the audience, smoking a cigarette. Throughout this scene sounds of shelling and explosions are heard in the distance.*

ALI: Welcome to Gaza. It is now 11:50 p.m. local occupation time. The temperature today is simmering, with white phosphorus showers expected. An umbrella will not help … nothing will.

MOHANAD *and* RAMI *crawl out of the tent.*

Thank you for choosing to travel with Ali's Tunnels. We hope you enjoyed our in-tunnel entertainment and hospitality.

The men look exhausted. They shake hands with ALI *and stand stretching their arms and legs.*

RAMI: My entertainment was in 3D: sight, sound and odour. I was crawling directly behind Mohanad.

MOHANAD: I told my wife that beans might not have been the best food to eat.

RAMI: Oh, is that what it was? I thought we were carrying biological weapons of mass destruction.

ALI: *Yallah shabab.* You should be grateful you no longer have to look at one another's butts.

RAMI: It's no use. After seven hours crawling behind Mohanad I can tell you his butt is now engraved in my mind.

ALI: I'll take you to my house first to get some rest, shower, and have a meal, and tomorrow morning we'll go to Shifa Hospital.

RAMI: No, Ali, I want to go straight to the hospital.

MOHANAD: We are anxious to roll up our sleeves and get to work. What are the numbers now?

ALI: Thousands in critical condition. Hundreds of dead, including many children. The doctors are puzzled by a strange kind of burning of the skin. They think it is caused by the white phosphorus bombs. It burns people from the inside out. Oh, and they blew up the mosque next to the hospital, so part of the hospital sustained damage and there is no glass on any of the windows.

RAMI: Let's go.

ALI: I have to warn you, our trip will be difficult. The shelling is random and merciless.

They start walking, looking around them in absolute horror. ALI *looks at his watch.*

Hey, pretty boy, give me a kiss. It is almost midnight.

RAMI: I'd rather you remain a frog ... Here comes 2009 with the most destructive fireworks ever. What a beautiful new year!

SCENE FIVE

Shifa Hospital, Gaza City.

Lots of injured people, some on beds, others on blankets on the floor. The place is buzzing with DOCTORS *and* NURSES. *There are periodic sounds of gunfire and missiles in the distance.*

A FATHER *and* MOTHER *are standing outside an operating room; the* MOTHER *is crying.*

RAMI *walks out of the operating room. His gloves and hospital uniform are stained with blood. He takes off the gloves and looks at them apologetically.*

RAMI: I am sorry. We lost him.

> *The* MOTHER *screams and falls down on her knees. The* FATHER *tries to help her but his knees give in too. They both sob on the floor.*

What is a life worth? This was the fifth child I lost today.
Damn it.
What is a life worth?
A grain of earth
A drop of oil
A flag on a hill of holy soil
A cross … a star … a crescent moon …
Is it worth ending a life too soon?
What sacred verses can explain
Sniper fire …
And white phosphorus rain?
What Holy Scripture gave the command
'Thou shall wipe out their villages
And scorch their land'?
And after the massacre
Will they lament
Will they seek forgiveness
Will they repent
Will they try to sanctify their burdened souls
For besieging a people behind their walls?

No rest for the less sacred, no safety, no light
No benediction, no prayer, no end in sight
No bread, no medicine, no shelter, no salvation
No angels can survive this holy Occupation
Tell me this:
What is a life worth
On this godforsaken earth?

  RAMI *walks offstage.*

  JOMANA *enters, carrying her phone. She sees the bereaved couple sobbing on the floor. She takes photos of them with her phone camera. They struggle back to their feet and walk offstage as* LAMA *enters.*

LAMA: Jomana!

  They run into each other's arms.

JOMANA: Lama! *Habibty,* you're a sight for sore eyes!

LAMA: I knew I'd find you here of all places.

JOMANA: Yes! Of all places! Here I am taking photos and doing interviews. Hoping that somehow I can compel the world to help us. Yes, we can be saved any minute now, my dear Lama … one more posting … one more status … one more tweet … wait and see … just one more photo is all it's going to take … one more dead baby and the world will rise. Don't worry; I know how delusional I really am. How is the camp?

LAMA: You are lucky your family left … it is like absolute hell, being there. I literally had to step over blood and human bits in the street on my way here.

JOMANA: How are you able to cope?

LAMA: By letting go of my sanity. Last night, while everyone in the house was hiding under beds and tables, something in me snapped. I found myself crawling out from under the kitchen table, and without even thinking I started making a *zaatar* sandwich. As the bombs fell around us my *zaatar* obsession got worse … and I was making more and more sandwiches. By the time the morning came, I found myself standing over the kitchen table along with my mother and my aunties and we were staring at a huge pile of *zaatar* sandwiches … It seems at some point during the night, that I can't even recall, the women in the family joined me. Can you imagine all four of us making sandwiches to the sound of bombs and sirens? I swear we are losing our minds.

JOMANA: Crazy is the 'in' thing now.

LAMA: So crazy we used up all the bread we had, which was supposed to last us till the end of the week.

JOMANA: So what will you do now?

LAMA: Does it matter? Does the rest of the week matter? Jomana, we can't even plan the next hour.

JOMANA: So what happened to the sandwiches?

LAMA: I came here and gave them out to the families who wait ... the ones waiting on the floor ... the ones waiting on the stairs ... the ones under the staircase ... Many refused them, some accepted them but with weary smiles ... but no-one really has an appetite.

ALI *enters, looking sombre.*

ALI: Lama ...

He holds LAMA*'s hand ... she starts to tremble.*

... may God give you strength and patience.

LAMA: No ... no ... no ... no ...

JOMANA: Who? Ali? Speak. Who?

ALI: 'To Allah we belong and to him we return' ... Your house was destroyed ... your parents and brothers have been martyred.

LAMA *screams and her knees give in.* JOMANA *and* ALI *stop her from falling.*

The SINGER *sings the song of mourning, 'Rahoo'.*

The lights fade out for a few moments. Only the voice of the SINGER *continues.*

When the lights come back on, JOMANA *is alone and frantically going from bed to bed looking at the faces of those injured. She sees a* NURSE.

JOMANA: Excuse me! Nurse, I heard the ambulance just brought in a family from Toffah. Can you tell me who they were?

NURSE: It was terrible. They're still bringing them in.

JOMANA: Who were they ... which family?

NURSE: I think they are from the Saleh family.

JOMANA *breathes a sigh of relief.*

JOMANA: Thank God … Oh, thank God! I mean, I'm sorry for the Saleh family, but I'm so glad … I thought my parents … Thank God …

The NURSE *leaves and the spotlight is now on* JOMANA *as everything around her fades into darkness.*

I have a confession to make
I stand between shame and relief
I breathe …
The missiles missed this time
Truth is they didn't really miss
Someone's house is destroyed
But not the house I know so well
Someone's family is grieving
But not the one whose name I carry
I linger …
I linger between shame and relief
I breathe …
I … breathe …
I tell myself
This flesh, torn and scattered
Is not flesh I have ever embraced
I soothe myself
Nor are these small lifeless hands
The ones with a crayon I've traced
I … breathe …
This time …
The missiles missed those
Whose names are engraved on my lips
This time they didn't stop those hearts
Beating in my chest
They live …
And I breathe …
But I must confess
Every time the bombs fall
I want answers
Where did they strike?
Which street did they blow up?

Which neighbourhood did they destroy?
Which lives did they steal?
Aware of my guilt I whisper a prayer
Dear God,
Please don't let it be the ones I know
Dear God
Please don't let it be the ones I love
Dear God …
Ya allah …
Ya allah …
Ya allah …
And when it's over
And while a less fortunate family weeps
I stand between shame and relief
I breathe …
I breathe …
Thank God my loved ones were spared …
This time!

> RAMI *enters and sees* JOMANA.

RAMI: Jomana!
JOMANA: Rami?

> *The two run into each other's arms,* JOMANA *sobbing.*

You're here … you're here … you're here …

> *The* SINGER *sings the song of lament,* 'Yamma moweel alhawa', *and continues to sing as the lights fade out and the next scene begins.*

SCENE SIX

Jomana's living room.

LAMA *and* JOMANA *are on the sofa, wearing black.* LAMA *has her head resting on* JOMANA's *lap.* JOMANA *is stroking her hair.*

LAMA: I feel so empty. It is all gone. Mama … Baba … Salim … Mahmoud …
JOMANA: Your family is in paradise.
LAMA: And I am in hell. I have nothing. No-one.

JOMANA: Don't say that. You have us.

The sounds of a funeral procession passing outside their home.

LAMA: I wonder whose funeral this is.

JOMANA: Either the Jaro or the Abu Shaban family. They both have funerals today.

LAMA: I am so sick of death.

A door knock, followed by ALI *walking in carrying two takeout boxes.*

ALI: *Ya sater.*

LAMA *sits up quickly and pulls her* hijab *over her hair.*

LAMA: You shouldn't have!

ALI: It's nothing. I wish there was something more I could do to make you smile again. But seeing I can't, at least let me ensure you don't waste away.

He hands her one box and gives the other to JOMANA.

Please promise me you will try to eat. Please, Lama … I can't stand the thought of anything happening to you.

JOMANA: Ali, why don't you join us?

ALI: I can't. We are trying to make the streets in the camp safe for passage. There is so much rubble and lots of dangerous explosives scattered all over the place … we have so much work to do.

LAMA: I heard you went to our house … what remains of our house … and you salvaged some of my family photos. I am grateful!

ALI: No need to be. I'm keeping them all in a box for you, you can go through them when you're feeling better. *Yallah*, I'll be back tonight. I don't want to see any food left then.

LAMA: Ali, please be careful. Promise me you'll be careful.

ALI *is touched by* LAMA*'s tenderness. He holds her hand and kisses it, then leaves.* JOMANA *opens* LAMA*'s box and hands her a piece of pita bread.*

JOMANA: *Yallah*, you heard the man. Eat!

LAMA: Whenever I see bread, I remember my last night with my family obsessing over *zaatar* sandwiches. It's as if we knew we had to use up all the bread before the house was blown up. It's strange when you think of your last moment with someone … standing across the kitchen table from my mom stuffing all the *zaatar* sandwiches into plastic bags ... I could have said so much to her if only I knew this was our last time together.

JOMANA: Lama ... *habibty* ...

LAMA: I miss her. I miss them all. I keep thinking at least my parents lived a full life. But my brothers, they were killed before they even had a life. They were handsome young men with so much left to do.

JOMANA: Yum! You should try these. They are the best *falafels* you can get in this city.

LAMA: They never got married or had children. Remember Salim's crush on Dalya?

JOMANA: The things he used to do just to catch a glimpse of her.

LAMA: I know. He was quite the Romeo. I wonder if he was still alive how his life would have been? Would he have married her? How many children would they have had?

JOMANA: Lama, there is no point in trying to imagine ... *Habibty*, he is in heaven now!

LAMA: He never even kissed her. Can you believe he had the chance a few times, but he never kissed her? Now he's dead. Jomana, I don't want this to happen to me. I don't want to die before I really know what life feels like.

JOMANA: Well, you will die if you don't eat. Come on, Lama, just try to take one bite. You need to start eating again.

LAMA: Do you know what I mean? Jomana, I am sick of death. I want to live, I want to love. I want to kiss someone ...

> JOMANA *looks at* LAMA *in shock.* LAMA *ignores* JOMANA*'s glare. She wills herself to bite into the sandwich. She chews with deliberate motion and then forces herself to swallow. She then looks at* JOMANA *with determination.*

Jomana. The mourning period of forty days is almost over. Soon there will be weddings in every neighbourhood in Gaza. I want my wedding to be one of them.

JOMANA: *What?!*

LAMA: I want to get married. I want to feel life growing inside of me. It is the only way I can defeat death ... by making life ... I want to have babies ... lots of babies ... I want to fill the house with their cries and laughter.

JOMANA: But, Lama, you weren't so sure about Ali …

LAMA: Things have become so much clearer now. Ali is a good man. He loves me. He stood by me through the worst days of my life. He would move mountains to see me smile. Besides, I can't wait for a romantic love story that may never be. A missile can fall from the sky tomorrow and we can all be dead. I simply will not postpone living anymore. Ali is a good provider and his tunnel business means we will never be hungry and we will never have to suffer the shortages.

JOMANA: But now? Are you sure you're ready now?

LAMA: I am sure this will save me.

> *A wedding drumbeat begins. The two girls leave the room.*
>
> ALI *and* RAMI *walk in, dressed in suits and carrying three photo frames: one of Lama's parents, and two of Lama's brothers. All three frames have a black ribbon across them.* ALI *and* RAMI *are in a joyful spirit. They are both laughing.*

RAMI: You finally did it!

ALI: Was it necessary for you and the thugs I call my cousins to manhandle me in the shower and to shave my …?

RAMI: We wanted to make sure the goods we deliver are not grotesque. Lord knows, it took forever to convince the poor girl to marry you.

ALI: Hey, don't believe these lies. She has chased after me for a long time. She is lucky I will let her have her way with me.

RAMI: So, what are we doing with these frames?

ALI: We will put them up at the wedding reception. We'll be hanging all the photos of those killed in both my family's and Lama's.

RAMI: I don't know how you do it.

ALI: If I were to define Gaza in two words, it would be funerals and weddings. You know, soon it will be your turn to have a wedding.

RAMI: *Inshallah.*

ALI: What is that about? Do I sense some doubt?

RAMI: I don't doubt my love for Jomana. But the more time I spend here, the more I'm convinced that I can't raise a family in this place.

ALI: Rami, here there is no room for grey comfort zones where we can have the luxury of indecision. When it comes to matters of the heart, in this place you have to know what you want and hold on to it for dear life.

RAMI: I want Jomana, but I want to take her away.

ALI: You want to uproot her? Sever her links with her family because you're too scared to live here?

RAMI: That's not fair. I am not scared for myself.

ALI: Brother, you have to be honest with yourself and with Jomana. It seems to me you are keeping one foot in this soil, and the other in some foreign land. Don't spend your whole life lost in between.

> ABU AHMED *enters, dressed in a suit.*

ABU AHMED: Ali, are you ready?

ALI: Yes, Uncle.

ABU AHMED: I don't have to tell you this, but I will. Lama is my daughter now, after my brother has been killed. So consider me your father-in-law and know that until the last day of my life, I will see to it that you are treating her with the love and respect she deserves.

ALI: I will. She is the love of my life. I will honour her forever.

> ABU AHMED *shakes hands with* ALI *and kisses him three times on the cheeks. He then turns to* RAMI, *gives him a quick look-over, and eyes his footwear.* RAMI *is relieved he is not wearing sandals with socks, but a nice pair of shoes.*

ABU AHMED: *Inshallah,* your turn will be next, doctor!

RAMI: *Inshallah!* I've been waiting for the right time to talk to you.

> ABU AHMED *and* RAMI *shake hands, and kiss in the same way, three kisses on the cheeks.*

ABU AHMED: I know. May God bring what is good for you and my daughter Jomana.

> *The sounds of* zaghroots *as* LAMA *and* JOMANA *enter.* LAMA *wears a white wedding dress and holds a plastic floral bouquet.* JOMANA *is behind her in a beautiful evening gown. They both look stunning.* JOMANA *lets out another* zaghroota.

> *The* SINGER *sings the traditional wedding song,* 'Qoolo la immoh tifra we tithana', *and continues to sing—lowering her voice when there is dialogue—until the end of this scene and into the next.*

JOMANA: *Ayeee* the groom is very lucky
Ayeee married into a great family
Ayeee Lama is a beautiful bride

Ayeee she is meant for Ali
Lolololololoyeeeee …

> *Everyone laughs.*

> *Suddenly the lights go out and everything is pitch dark for a few seconds.* ALI *lights up the room with his cell phone until* JOMANA *turns on the lantern. She takes the flowers out of* LAMA*'s hand and puts them on the table, giving* LAMA *the lantern to hold instead.*

This is more useful now.

> *Holding the lantern,* LAMA *takes in a deep breath, looks at* ALI *and smiles.* ALI *walks over to her and lifts her veil.*

ALI: I am the luckiest man in the world. I will devote my life to making you happy.

> *He kisses* LAMA *on her forehead then holds her hand and looks at her, smiling.*

Are you ready?

LAMA: I am! I've never been more ready in my life. You are a good man, Ali, and I am lucky to have you.

> *The procession begins to move with* ALI *and* LAMA *in the front holding the lantern and the lights fade out while the* SINGER *continues to sing into the next scene.*

SCENE SEVEN

Gaza beach.

JOMANA *and* RAMI *walk, holding hands.*

JOMANA: Here we are … we keep finding ourselves in the same place.

RAMI: I can't believe a year has passed since we first met.

JOMANA: Don't tell me a year has passed. You can't measure our lives by a calendar. Time stands still here.

RAMI: Frozen on the shores of this old battered city.

JOMANA: One calendar year can never contain our lives, our sorrows, desires …

RAMI: Then let us be lost in the absence of time and linger in this moment forever.

He holds her and kisses her on the lips. She pulls away slowly.

JOMANA: You are fully taking advantage of our engagement.

RAMI: Not fully! Not yet!

He pulls her closer one more time. They have one long kiss.
JOMANA *pushes him away slowly and looks around, worried.*

JOMANA: You know we can get arrested for this.

RAMI: Arrested for kissing?

JOMANA *steps away.*

This place keeps growing on me every day.

JOMANA: What was that?

RAMI: I'm just so sick of this … the waiting. Remind me why are we not married yet?

JOMANA: Because you still need to go back to Texas and close your clinic and move your things.

RAMI: No, I mean why are we waiting? Let's just have the wedding and then you can come with me to Texas—it's a great place. You would love it there. You know, kissing is actually celebrated not criminalised in that part of the world.

JOMANA: Well then, let's go!

RAMI: I am serious. I want us to get married now and leave … both of us … together.

JOMANA: Leave? We've talked about this. You promised me we would stay here. I can't leave. If I leave I may never see my family again.

RAMI: Well, what about my family? My mother can't come here. What about her right to be with her grandchildren? What about my sisters, my friends … my practice … what about our future children … don't they have the right to the best education, the best environment and the best life?

JOMANA: What exactly is this about? You promised me we would stay here … I thought we had a plan.

RAMI: Plans don't work in this environment of uncertainty.

JOMANA: I would have never allowed myself to get so close to you if I knew you planned to uproot me. You promised …

RAMI: I did. But that was before I knew what it was like to live here. Now I know.

JOMANA: Now you know? They tried to warn me, but I didn't want to listen. My father told me your roots were not dug deep in this soil. I told him I had faith in you …

> JOMANA *turns around and tries to leave, but* RAMI *pulls her back.*

RAMI: Stop. Jomana, stop. I need you to hear me.

> *She pulls her hand angrily and tries to leave again, but he yells:*

Jomana, you must hear me!

> *She stops.*

You know I would go to the moon for you. I love you. But you have to understand we are talking about marriage and raising a family … here. This complicates things. Since I've come here, I've treated hundreds of children with bullet wounds, shrapnel, white phosphorus burns, explosives … I keep wondering: What if I have children here? What if one day, my own child is brought to me on a stretcher? How do I protect my family here from this sky that rains death? What if the woman I love—?

JOMANA: Don't 'what if…?' Rami, my life is here. My family is here. I was raised here. This place is my home.

RAMI: This place is a prison. You are trapped behind a big wall. Do you really want to condemn our children to this fate? I want a better life for us, for our children.

JOMANA: Yes, we are trapped behind a wall, but Rami, look around you. Open your eyes. See all the stories of how we survive; the trees we've replanted, the homes we've rebuilt. Inside these walls, Rami, old men still fiddle with their prayer beads. Mothers still bake *maamoul* on *Eid*. Families still gather under canopies with loaded bunches of grapes dangling above their heads, they nibble on watermelon seeds and drink *maramiah* tea. Women still perfect the art of matchmaking. Men still dream of freedom and democracy. Children climb on almond trees. Lovers woo in secrecy. And no matter how the conditions are adverse, over here we have learned to defy the universe! Every day inside these walls, Rami, we defy the universe!

RAMI: I don't know how you do that. I can't … I'm not used to this …

JOMANA: I know it is not easy for you. You have a life out there that I can't even imagine. But my life is right here. My life is right here.

RAMI: This has been a very difficult year.

JOMANA: I know! Rami, we've been through hell this year. I know that neither one of us is the same person we were that day on the beach a year ago. I'm not the same woman that begged you to stay. I really do understand … So if you have doubts …

RAMI: I don't doubt my love for you.

JOMANA: You are free to leave.

RAMI: I can't live without you.

He wraps his arms around her; she rests her head on his shoulder.

I can't live without you.

JOMANA: So what now?

RAMI: I will come back. I'll finish my work in the US as fast as I can and I will come back. I promise

The SINGER *sings the farewell song, 'Ma'a el salameh', and the lights fade out. The* SINGER *continues the song into the next scene.*

SCENE EIGHT

An airport lounge somewhere in United States.

RAMI *on the phone talking to* SAMIRA. *Two* HOMELAND SECURITY OFFICERS *stand a few steps away from him, watching.*

RAMI: Hi, Mom, just one last plane and I'll be home. You won't believe how many random checks I was subjected to. They've just made a final boarding announcement, I'm going in. Just remember, don't prepare any Arabic food for me … I've had way too much of it this past year … What I really miss is your hearty chilli con carne. Spice it up, Mom! *Yallah*, I'll see you soon. I love you.

RAMI *stands with his ticket in his hand. He takes a look around and smiles.*

Finally! Home sweet home!

The two OFFICERS *approach him.*

OFFICER 1: I'm sorry, sir, you've been selected for an extra random security check.

RAMI: No kidding! Again? I am curious, how random can a random check be when it is consistently applied?

OFFICER 2: Please remain calm. This won't take long.

> SAMIRA, *appears standing to the side, watching* RAMI *with a gentle beautiful smile. She is not visible to the* OFFICERS. *She remains there throughout the scene.*

> RAMI *smiles back at her.*

> RAMI *reads the refrain from 'Green Eggs and Ham' by Dr Seuss.*

OFFICER 1: Sir?

RAMI: [*to the* OFFICERS] I have brown skin and I don't eat ham,
  Whenever I fly … random I am …

OFFICER 2: Sir, we need you to step aside.

OFFICER 1: We must search you.

RAMI: I have nothing to hide.
  I have brown skin and I don't eat ham,
  Whenever I travel … random I am …

OFFICER 1: Would you spread your legs?

OFFICER 2: Roll up your shirt.

OFFICER 1: Stretch out your arms.

OFFICER 2: This won't hurt.

RAMI: I would spread my legs,
  Roll up my shirt,
  Stretch out my arms,
  And this does hurt.
  I have brown skin and I don't eat ham,
  So once again … random I am …

OFFICER 1: Would you, could you, say why you're here?

OFFICER 2: Would you, could you, calm our fear?

RAMI: I would and have at every gate,
  Please let me go, I don't want to be late,
  I'm constantly selected to step aside,
  Photographed, fingerprinted, I've nothing to hide.
  I've spread my legs, rolled up my shirt,
  I've stretched my arms, in spite of the hurt,
  I have brown skin and I don't eat ham,
  I am an Arab … so random I am.

OFFICER 1: Why are you here?

RAMI: I am an American citizen on my way home.

OFFICER 2: Why would an American visit a place like Gaza?

RAMI: To marry the woman I love …

OFFICER 1: And where is she?

RAMI: Still in Gaza. Look, officer, is there a reason for this interrogation? I'm going to miss my flight.

OFFICER 2: How did you get into Gaza?

RAMI: I …

OFFICER 1: Your passport has no entry stamp into Gaza, only an exit one. So … we're curious … how did you get in?

RAMI: Where is this going?

OFFICER 2: You know Hamas is a listed terrorist organisation in the US.

RAMI: Of course I know.

OFFICER 1: Yet you used illegal underground tunnels to get into Hamas territory? You are under arrest for having links with a terrorist organisation.

RAMI: I demand a lawyer.

OFFICER 2: You need one. This is a matter of great national security.

The SINGER *sings the prison song,* 'Ya thalam alsijin khayem '.

The lights fade out and only the SINGER'*s voice continues into the next scene.*

SCENE NINE

Gaza beach.

JOMANA *sits, holding her diary. The sound of waves in the background.*
ALI *and* LAMA *enter, holding hands.* LAMA, *visibly pregnant, is wearing a maternity dress. They sit next to* JOMANA *and all three stare into the horizon.*

ALI: Still no news from Rami?

JOMANA: His mother has assigned him good lawyers, but I think it will take a long time. It is not clear who will be freed first, him or this old city.

LAMA: Why don't you come and spend the day with us? We miss our chaperone!

ALI: No offence, but I don't miss the chaperone so much.

JOMANA: Come on, Ali, you had it easy.

ALI: I did. Thank you.

LAMA: We are going to the zoo to see the zebra.

JOMANA: You mean the donkey that was spray-painted to look like a zebra?

ALI: Shhh! Don't ruin it.

JOMANA: It is nice to see you, Lama, so glowing and so happy.

ALI: There is more to this place than broken hearts and tragic tales.

LAMA: [*touching her belly*] There is life here!

> JOMANA *looks at* ALI *holding* LAMA*'s hand.*

JOMANA: There is so much love here.

LAMA: I only wish you could have that.

JOMANA: But I do! My heart is so filled with love … and an infinite amount of patience!

> *She stands up, holding her diary. She takes a few steps away from the couple. The spotlight follows her.*

The landscape constantly changes
Only the sea remains
A cure for the trail of broken lives left behind
A landmark untouched by human greed and destruction
Oblivious to war, occupation and aggression
Defiant to the rules of man.

There is no end to the sea's audacity
It breaks the siege every day
One defiant wave at a time
The landscape will change
Only the sea will remain
Its whooshing waves will whisper new tales
Of occupiers that have come
And gone.

> *The* SINGER *sings the sea song,* 'Haddy ya baher haddy'.
>
> *The lights gently fade out.*

THE END

GLOSSARY OF ARABIC WORDS AND TERMS

All translations are from standard Arabic usage unless noted otherwise.

'To Allah we belong and to him we return' – a verse from the Quran often used in condolences

ahleen – welcome

Ammu – Uncle

Ayeee – the beginning of a traditional wedding rhyme, often followed by group *zaghrootas* or ululation

Baba – Father

baklava – sweet pastry containing nuts

debka – traditional Palestinian step dancing

Eid al-Fitr – the festival and feast which marks the end of the Ramadan month of fasting

falafel – a deep-fried ball of ground chickpeas and spices

habibty – my love, darling or sweetheart

hijab – a traditional headscarf worn by Muslim women, covering the hair, neck and shoulders

Inshallah – If God wills it

keffieh – a traditional headdress worn by Arab men; wearing a chequered black-and-white *keffieh* over the shoulders is a symbol of solidarity with the Palestinian cause

khalas – okay, enough

Khalto – Auntie

kunafa – sweet cheese pastry

maamoul – cookies stuffed with dates and nuts

maramiah – sage

merhaba – a common Palestinian greeting

sheesha – water pipe for smoking

shokran – thank you

tarbush – a brimless felt cap, usually red, with a silk tassel; worn by some Middle-Eastern men, especially in the early 1900s

tayeb – fine

ya alby – my heart; a term of endearment

ya allah – Oh, God!

ya sater – a Gazan expression used by men to announce their arrival

yallah – the equivalent to saying Come on! or Hurry up!

yallah shabab – the equivalent to saying Come on guys or Let's go guys

zaatar – thyme and olive oil on bread

zaghroota – a joyful sound traditionally made by Middle-Eastern women at weddings

www.ingramcontent.com/pod-product-compliance
Lightning Source LLC
Chambersburg PA
CBHW050027090426
42734CB00021B/3458